THINK
OUTSIDE
THE BOX

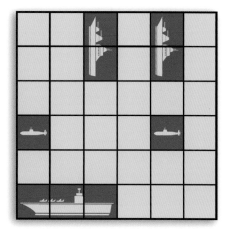

Thanks to the creative team:

Senior Editor: Alice Peebles

Designer: Bryony Anne Warren and Collaborate Agency

First American edition published in 2015 by Lerner Publishing Group, Inc.

Hungry Tomato™
A division of Lerner Publishing Group, Inc.
241 First Avenue North
Minneapolis, MN 55401 USA

For reading levels and more information, look up this title
at www.lernerbooks.com.

Library of Congress Cataloging-in-Publication Data

Moore, Gareth.
    Think outside the box / Dr. Gareth Moore.
       pages cm. — (Brain benders)
    ISBN 978-1-4677-6344-8 (lb : alk. paper) — ISBN 978-1-4677-7205-1
(pb: alk. paper) — ISBN 978-1-4677-7206-8 (eb pdf)
    1. Shapes—Juvenile literature. 2. Picture puzzles—Juvenile literature.
I. Title.
QA445.5.M66 2015
516'.15—dc23   2015001582

Manufactured in the United States of America
1 – VP – 7/15/15

BrAiN BENDERS

THINK OUTSIDE THE BOX

by Dr. Gareth Moore

HUNGRY TOMATO™

MINNEAPOLIS

Contents

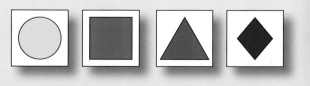

Think Outside the Box

Get ready to use your imagination with mind-bending puzzles and games! If you get stuck, you'll find hints in the back of the book, along with the answers to each challenge. But here's the biggest secret: learn to think outside the box!

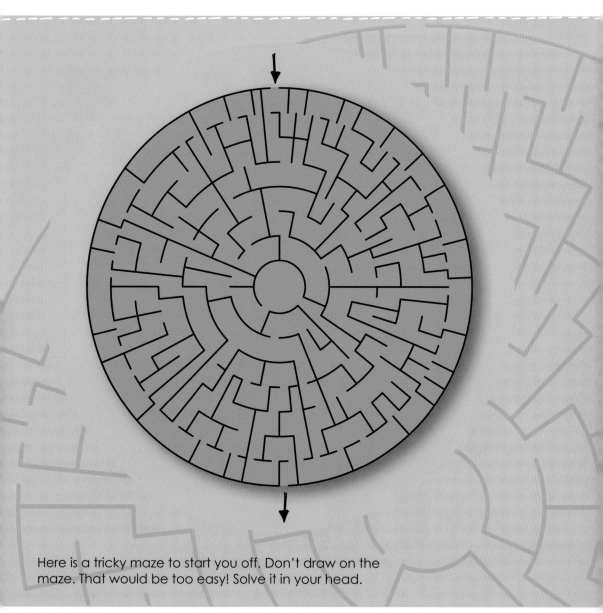

Here is a tricky maze to start you off. Don't draw on the maze. That would be too easy! Solve it in your head.

Need help with solving a puzzle? Turn to pages 26–29 for helpful tips.

Seeing It in Your Head

You might not be able to move things around the room with just the power of your mind, but you can still imagine what it would look like if you could! Let's test out the power of your imagination with these shape puzzles.

1 Sliding around

Look at these six tiles. Imagine sliding them around to new positions. What letter can you make?

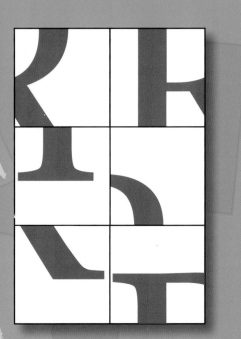

Now try these six tiles. What letter can you make if you rearrange them?

2 Shape combination

Combine these pictures with the power of your mind! If you remove the white squares from one picture and put that picture on top of the other one, how many stars can you count?

3 Stacking things up

Imagine you have four colored tiles, A, B, C, and D, as shown here, and each is printed on a piece of clear plastic. What order would you stack them in to make each of the three pictures below?

For example, if you put down D and then put C on top, you'll end up with a yellow oval on top of a blue rectangle.

A   B

C   D

1   2   3

Need help with solving a puzzle? Turn to pages 26–29 for helpful tips.

7

Shape Fitting

Have you ever built a model, either from a kit or using your imagination? How good are you at putting things together just in your head? Here's a chance to find out!

1 Cutting it up

This pattern has been cut up into **four** identical pieces. Some of them have been rotated, but they're all the same shape.

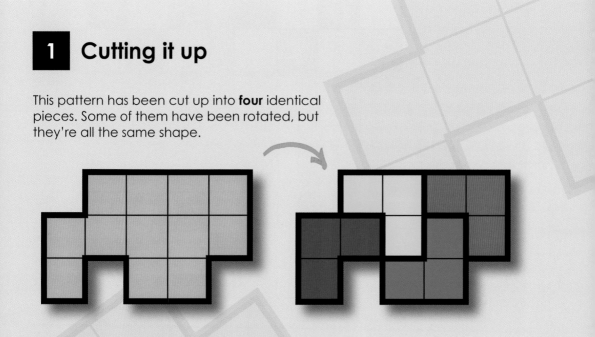

Use your imagination to figure out how to cut each of the following patterns into **four** identical shapes.

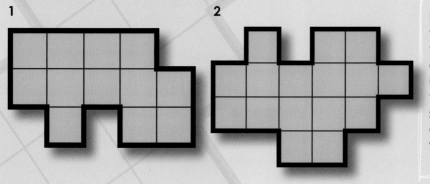

If you get stuck, you can copy the patterns on paper and use a pencil to trace the shapes, but try doing them in your head!

2 Cracking problem

Two of these pieces can be put together to make a whole egg, without any gaps. Can you figure out which two?

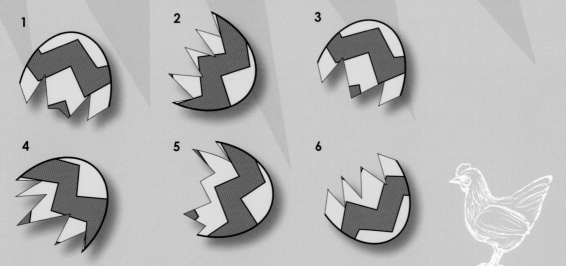

1   2   3

4   5   6

3 Access granted

Which of the numbered shapes exactly fits with the shape of the key shown here?

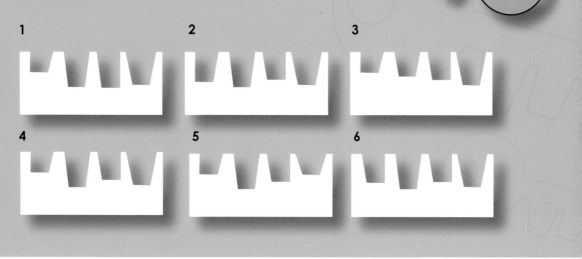

1   2   3

4   5   6

Need help with solving a puzzle? Turn to pages 26–29 for helpful tips.

Games for One

Have you ever played tic-tac-toe or battleship with a friend? Try these solo versions for just one player – no friend required! You'll still need a pen and paper, not to mention your thinking cap.

1 Solo tic-tac-toe

In two-player tic-tac-toe, the aim is to get three Xs or three Os in a line. Here the aim is to **never** get **four** Xs or Os in a line.

Just like the two-player game, lines can run in any direction, including diagonally. Start by copying every grid exactly as shown here. To play, you need to write an O or an X in every empty box without creating any lines of four.

Unlike the two-player game, you don't need to alternate writing X's and O's, so you might have more of one symbol than the other in the finished puzzle.

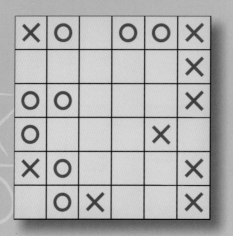

2 Solo battleship

Two-player battleship involves finding the other player's fleet of ships on the grid. And two ships can't touch each other, not even diagonally. This one-player version works the same way, except you get some clues about where the ships are.

The numbers at the end of each row and column tell you how many squares in that row or column contain part of a ship.

Here's an example of a completed puzzle, where all of the ships have been found.

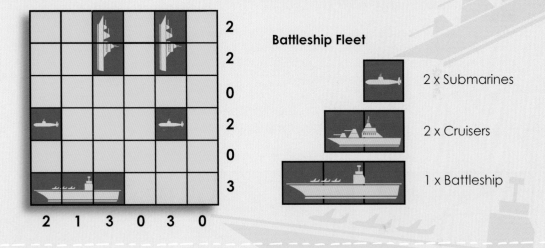

Battleship Fleet

2 x Submarines

2 x Cruisers

1 x Battleship

Copy each battleship grid, including the numbers next to it. Then try to find each of the listed ships on the grid. You can do this by thinking, not just randomly guessing.

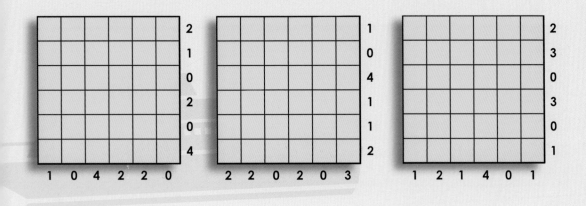

Need help with solving a puzzle? Turn to pages 26–29 for helpful tips.

(11)

An Unusual View

Do you notice the small details in the world around you, such as the pattern on a football player's jersey or the writing on the side of a pen? These pages are all about small details.

1 Close-up imagination

Have you ever made up a story? See what you can make up for each of these pictures. Each image is a close-up view of something. What do you think the big picture might be?

For example, the first one could be the trunk and ear of an elephant lying on its back! What do **you** see when you look at these pictures?

2

Close-up details

Look at these close-up pictures of everyday objects.
You've probably seen or used all of these items before.

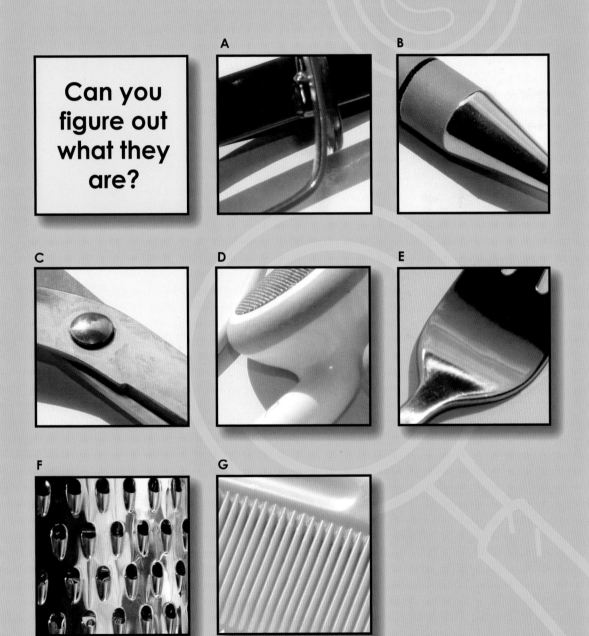

A
B
C
D
E
F
G

Can you figure out what they are?

Need help with solving a puzzle? Turn to pages 26–29 for helpful tips.

(13)

Around and About

Have you ever tried reading a map? It can sometimes be pretty tough to figure out which way is left or right from your point of view. These puzzles will help you practice those skills.

1 Rotated all round

Rotate each picture in the direction shown by the arrow beneath it. In other words, you rotate the first picture by a quarter of a turn clockwise, the second picture by a half turn, and the third picture by a quarter turn counterclockwise.

Which of the options below – A, B, or C – would work in each case?

2 On reflection

If you look in a mirror and wave your right hand, in the reflection it looks like it's your left hand waving. Can you imagine what other things would look like if seen in a mirror?

On a piece of paper, draw what you'd see if you held up each of these patterns in front of a mirror. Then fold your paper along the edge of your drawing and line it up against the edge of the pattern in the book. Have you drawn the reflection correctly? If you have, you'll reveal a simple picture!

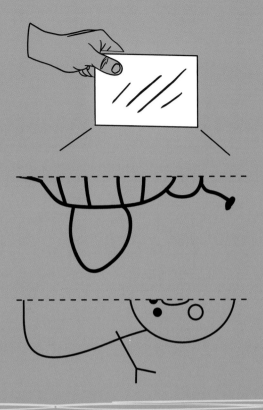

3 Mirror writing

Have you ever tried looking at your handwriting in a mirror? It can be pretty hard to read! Can you figure out what has been written here? Then see if you can write out your name so that it would be readable if you viewed it in a mirror. It's a lot trickier than you'd think!

Finally, try copying these stick people on a piece of paper so that they would look the same when reflected in a mirror.

Need help with solving a puzzle? Turn to pages 26–29 for helpful tips.

(15)

3D Cubes

Have you ever tried drawing a picture of a three-dimensional object? You need to somehow show the different distances you see with your eyes in a completely flat drawing on a piece of paper. It can be pretty tricky, but in these puzzles you'll do the opposite, which can be even trickier. You'll think about how some drawings would look if they were real objects right in front of you.

1 Counting cubes

Look at this picture of some cubes. You can only directly see four cubes, but there must be a fifth one under there to stop the one on top from falling down.

Now imagine that you start with an arrangement of cubes like the one in this picture. It is made up of 27 cubes, with three layers that have nine cubes each.

Imagine that you now take away some of the cubes and end up with this picture. How many cubes are left in the arrangement?

And how many cubes are in the arrangement on the far right?

Imagine that you have an arrangement of 64 cubes set up like this, with 16 cubes in each of four layers.

If you start from this point each time, how many cubes must be in each of the following pictures?

2 Folding cubes

Imagine what would happen if you cut out each of these patterns and folded along the lines. Most of the patterns can be folded up to make a perfect cube, with a solid surface on all six sides, but there are three exceptions. Which patterns are the three odd ones out?

Thinking in 3D

Do you have the power to build things entirely in your mind? These objects are all flat drawings, but you can use your imagination to figure out what they would look like if they were solid objects.

1 Odd cube out

Without actually trying it out, imagine that you've cut out each of these four patterns and then folded along the lines to make cubes. Three of them would be identical, but one would be different. Which one?

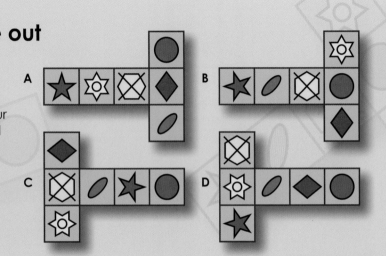

2 Pyramid power

The ancient Egyptians built pyramids – and so can you, using just your brainpower! Imagine that each of these shape templates had been cut out and folded along the lines. Only two would make a four-sided pyramid without any missing sides – but which two would work?

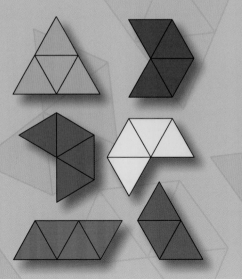

3 Pop-up cubes

Have you ever tried drawing a picture of a cube where all the edges are visible, even the ones that should be out of sight? This is called a wireframe cube.

Check out the red wireframe cube below. Do you see it as a cube that sits out to the front and left, as in the first blue picture, or as a cube that lifts up and to the right, as in the second blue picture? An X marks the front of each cube, to help you see the difference between the images.

By looking at the red wireframe cube carefully, can you swap back and forth between both versions of the cube and see it both ways? It can take some practice, but you can do it! You probably find the left-hand version easier to see, because you're more used to looking down on a cube-shaped object, such as a building block or a die, rather than looking up at it. To see the right-hand view with a real cube, you'd need to hold the cube above your eyes or look up at it from under a table with a clear surface.

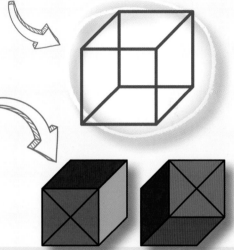

4 Even more pop-up cubes

In the left-hand picture, can you see a cube that you are looking down on from above? Can you also see a cube that you are looking up at from below? Both are there, but it might take you a bit longer to see the one from below. Keep trying – sooner or later it will pop up in front of you!

If you managed that, try the image on the right. It isn't obvious that this simple picture hides two cubes! What's amazing is that this is just a regular hexagon with lines joining all of the opposite corners. Try drawing this out for yourself.

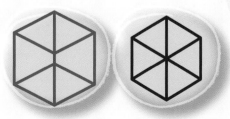

Need help with solving a puzzle? Turn to pages 26–29 for helpful tips.

Confusing Lines

You'll need to concentrate to solve the mazes on these pages. Solve them in your head or use a finger to trace your path. Don't draw on a maze – that's cheating!

1 Circular maze

Can you find your way through this circular maze? Enter at the top and then make your way through until you come out at the bottom. Be careful, because the twisting paths make it easy to get stuck!

2 Bridge mazes

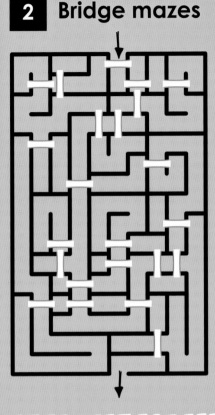

Real-life mazes sometimes have bridges that you can use to cross over the paths. The mazes on this page are just like that, with bridges where one path crosses over another. Don't forget that you can go underneath these bridges too!

If you get stuck, retrace your steps and make sure you haven't missed a route over or under a bridge.

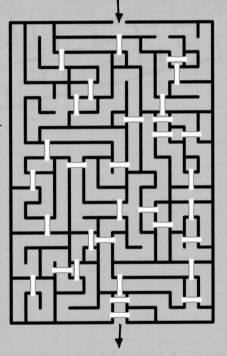

3 Hidden star

Can you find this star shape in this maze of lines? It may appear at a different angle and size, but it will otherwise look exactly the same.

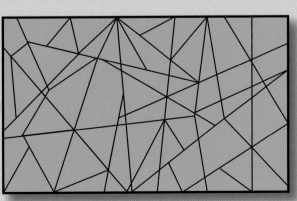

Need help with solving a puzzle? Turn to pages 26–29 for helpful tips.

21

Hidden in Plain Sight

Military vehicles and soldiers use camouflage to make them hard to spot in battle, and many animals are colored or patterned to help them blend in with their natural environments. You can become a camouflage expert too. Can you find all of the carefully hidden objects on these pages?

1 Squaring the circle

This circle of dots hides a square! Can you figure out how you could fit a square over the top of these dots, so that all of the dots lie somewhere on the edge of the square? It might look impossible, but it's not!

2 Counting conundrum

This big rectangle is made up of lots of little rectangles. How many rectangles can you count by tracing along the lines? Don't forget to count the big rectangle, too!

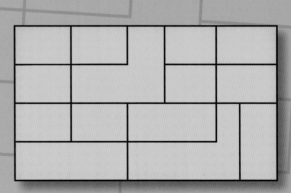

3

Secret writing

This might look like just a page of random typed letters, but try putting the book down and looking at it from a distance. What can you see now?

Need help with solving a puzzle? Turn to pages 26–29 for helpful tips.

23

Logic Challenges

It's amazing what you can do when you stop and think. All of the puzzles on these pages will be hard if you try to solve them by guessing, but if you use logic and strategy, you'll find they're a lot easier than they look!

1 Rows and columns

A Latin square is a square grid where exactly the same set of items appears once in every row and column. Grids like this have been used for thousands of years, sometimes just as decoration. The puzzles on this page will challenge you to fill square grids with shapes to make Latin squares of your own.

Here are the four shapes to use

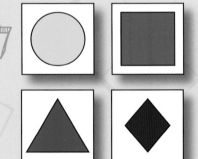

Start by copying the first of these three grids onto a piece of paper. Copy and cut out the shapes too. (You don't have to color the shapes unless you want to.) Can you fill all the empty squares so that each of the four shapes appears exactly once in every row and column? Then try the other two puzzles. Each one is a little harder than the last.

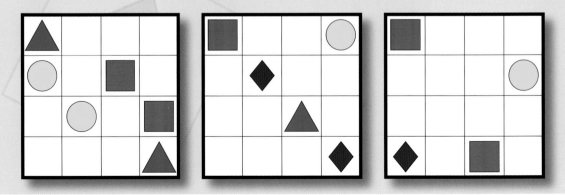

2 Extra regions, rows, and columns

With these puzzles, your mission is to place one of each shape in each of the bold-lined regions. The finished grid still needs to form a Latin square, but now you must work with these extra regions, too.

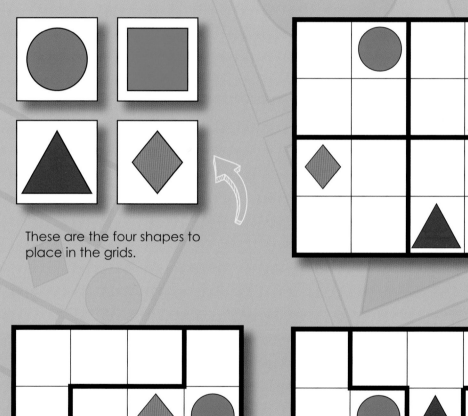

These are the four shapes to place in the grids.

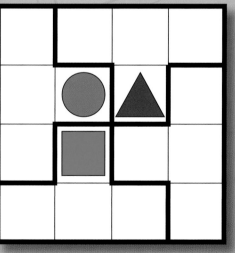

Helpful Tips

Page 5
Think Outside the Box
See page 28 for hint.

Pages 6 – 7
Seeing it in Your Head

Sliding around

Some of the pieces contain part of an image that continues off to the right, while others continue to the left, or up, or down. With this in mind, imagine how they fit together. Think through each of the capital letters in the alphabet until you find one that fits.

Shape combination

Count the stars you see on one half of the puzzle, even if you can only see a bit of each one. Then, on the other half of the puzzle, you only need to add the stars that sit entirely within a square.

Stacking things up

Look for the color that's at the back. That's your first layer. Then find a color that's on top of that one but beneath the other two.

Pages 8 – 9
Shape Fitting

Cutting it up

Start by counting the number of grid squares. Divide that number by four to find how many squares are in each piece. Then you can look for bits of the pattern that stick out where you know two squares must go together.

Cracking problem

Use a process of elimination. Pick any half and see if another half fits. If not, you can forget about the half you are looking at and move on.

Access granted

This is a spot-the-difference puzzle with six options. The spaces in the key will match the outline of one shape. Compare each shape in turn with the key, checking each gap between the teeth.

Pages 10 – 11
Games for One

Solo tic-tac-toe

Start by looking for any square that would make a line of four Os if it had an O in it. If you find one, then it has to have an X in it to avoid a line of four. Then check again for the opposite: squares that must have an O because an X would make a full line.

Solo battleship

The key to this puzzle is to mark not just the ships but also the "misses" —the squares you know must contain water.

Start with the rows and columns marked O and put an X in every square to mark a "miss." Now, are there any rows or columns where the number of ship segments equals the number of non-"miss" squares? If so, you can fill these in.

Next, look at the list of ships you have to find. Is there only one place in the grid where one of these ships will fit? If so, fill it in!

Pages 12 – 13
An Unusual View
Close-up imagination

There are no "correct" answers here! You can always invent things if you can't think of anything real, so if you want something to be a monster from outer space, that's fine!

Close-up details

If you're stuck, ask a friend to help! Sometimes what's hidden to you is obvious to others. Here are some clues about the objects:

- You use one of them in your hair.
- Two of them can be found in a kitchen.
- Two of them are writing tools.
- You might put one of them in your ears.
- One of them might rest on your nose!

Pages 14 – 15
Around and About
Rotated all round

Look for the differences among the three options, and then think about which of these differences would be the one that matches the original.

On reflection

You might find it easier to copy these accurately if you start by tracing the beginning and end of the edges of each drawing onto a piece of paper. This will help you make sure you start drawing at the same size, so the result is more likely to line up.

Mirror writing

Write your name normally first. Then look at it in a mirror and try copying it from there. Then cover that over and see if you can do it again without help! You can use a similar process with the stick people.

Pages 16 – 17
3D Cubes
Counting cubes

The secret is being organized by treating each layer in turn as a smaller, easier puzzle. Count all of the cubes in just the top layer and write down that number. Then repeat for each of the layers, and add up all of the layer totals to get your overall answer. When counting, don't forget to include the "hidden" cubes that you can't see. That's part of the challenge.

Folding cubes

One thing you might notice right away is that some of the patterns are very similar. For example, any that are made up of four

squares in a straight line, with one square sticking off to either side, will definitely make a cube.

Imagine the four squares wrapping around in a loop, and then the other two squares folding up as flaps to complete the cube.

If you're really stuck, you can copy the patterns on paper, carefully cut them out, and fold them up to see what happens.

Thinking in 3D

Odd cube out

Each of the unfolded cubes has the same six shapes on it, so one way to solve this puzzle is to pick each of the six shapes in turn and think about how that shape would appear next to the other cubes. Think about both the shape's position on the cube and whether it has been moved or not.

Pyramid power

You can eliminate the green choice right away because it only has three sides, not four. The others are trickier to think about, but you can make it easier by noticing that the yellow, blue, and purple choices are all exactly the same.

Pop-up cubes

Try looking back and forth between the wireframe cube and the solid blue cubes. This can help you focus on the parts of the image that will let you see the cubes in both ways.

Even more pop-up cubes

Try drawing out solid versions of the cubes if you find this tricky. Then look back and forth between these and the wireframes. You could also pick up an actual cube, such as a building block or a die, and compare it with the drawn cubes.

Pages 5, 20 – 21

Confusing Lines

Circular maze

You can't use a pen or a pencil to draw on the maze, so the secret is to use your memory instead! Each time you reach a turn, try to remember the option you picked, so that if you go wrong you can avoid repeating the same mistake next time!

Bridge mazes

This path can travel over and under itself, so you can't assume that you need to move in the direction of the exit at all times. Sometimes the correct route may appear to be going in the wrong direction!

Hidden star

Remember that the star may be a different size, and perhaps rotated at a different angle than the yellow picture. If you're still stuck, pay attention to the left-hand side of the drawing.

Pages 22 – 23

Hidden in Plain Sight

Squaring the circle

You know you are looking for a square, and you have eight dots. You also know that squares have four straight sides, which means that at least four pairs of the dots must be linked by straight lines. Imagine this as a dot-to-dot puzzle with the four corner dots all missing!

Counting conundrum

Consider each corner in turn, from left to right and top to bottom, and then count the number of rectangles that use each corner. Each rectangle has four corners, so if you do this for every corner in the picture you'll end up counting each rectangle four times. Just divide your total count by four to get the answer. Another method is to make sure you only count each rectangle once, so for each corner in the picture you should only count the rectangles that share their top-left corners with that particular outer corner. This will help you make sure you only count each rectangle once, since of course each rectangle only has one top-left corner!

Secret writing

If you can't see it, step as far away from the book as you can and look again. Can you see it now? It's an animal's face.

Pages 24 – 25
Logic Challenges

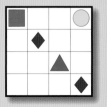

Rows and columns

Consider each row and column – what shapes are missing? For each missing shape, see which empty squares it can fit in without repeating the shape in a row or a column. If there's only one fit, place it! Another option is to pick an empty square and work through the shapes that might fit in it – and if there's only one possibility, fill it in!

Extra regions, rows, and columns

Use the tips for "Rows and columns" on the left, but also check the regions. Look in each region to see what shapes are still missing, and if there's only one place you can fit a particular shape, fill it in!

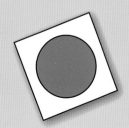

Answers

Page 5 Think Outside the Box

Pages 6 – 7 Seeing It in Your Head

Sliding around

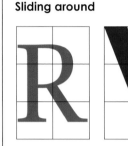

Shape combination

There are 15 stars.

Stacking things up

1) BDCA   2) ACDB   3) DBCA

Pages 8 – 9
Shape Fitting

Cutting it up

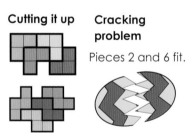

Cracking problem

Pieces 2 and 6 fit.

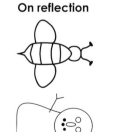

Access granted

Shape 4 matches.

Pages 10 – 11
Games for One

Solo tic-tac-toe

×	O	×	O
O	O	×	×
×	O	O	O
O	×	O	×

×	O	×	O	O	×
×	O	×	O	×	×
O	O	×	O	×	O
O	×	O	×	O	×
×	O	×	O	O	×
×	O	×	O	O	×

O	×	O	O	O
O	×	×	×	O
×	O	O	O	×
×	O	×	×	O
O	×	×	×	O

Solo battleship

Page 13
An Unusual View

Close-up details

A) a pair of glasses

B) a pen

C) a pair of scissors

D) earphones

E) a fork

F) a grater

G) a comb

Pages 14 – 15 Around and About

Rotated all around

1) B

2) A

3) C

Mirror writing

The text says "Mirror writing."

On reflection

Pages 16 – 17 3D Cubes

Counting cubes

a) 16 cubes: 4 in layer 1, 5 in layer 2, 7 in layer 3

b) 11 cubes: 2 in layer 1, 2 in layer 2, 7 in layer 3

c) 33 cubes: 4 in layer 1, 6 in layer 2, 9 in layer 3, 14 in layer 4

d) 23 cubes: 1 in layer 1, 4 in layer 2, 6 in layer 3, 12 in layer 4

Folding cubes

Pages 18

Thinking in 3D

Odd cube out

C is different. The pink oval is rotated compared to the other cubes.

Pyramid power

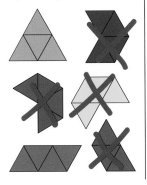

Pages 20 – 21 **Confusing Lines**

Circular maze

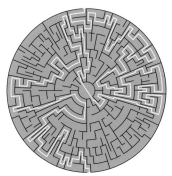

Hidden star

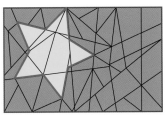

Bridge mazes

Pages 22 – 23 **Hidden in Plain Sight**

Squaring the circle

Counting conundrum

Counting the larger rectangles as well as smaller ones inside them, you should get a total of 33.

Secret writing

Pages 24 – 25 **Logic Challenges**

Rows and columns

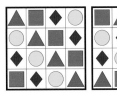

Extra regions, rows, and columns

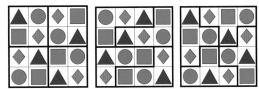

Index

About the Author

Dr. Gareth Moore is the author of a wide range of puzzle and brain-training books for both children and adults, including *The Kids' Book of Puzzles, The Mammoth Book of Brain Games,* and *The Rough Guide Book of Brain Training*. He is also the founder of daily brain training site **www.BrainedUp.com**. He earned his Ph.D from Cambridge University (UK) in the field of computer speech recognition, teaching machines to understand spoken words.